T0198524

Shadows, Shades, and Brilliant Light

MY STORY

ELAINE LEWIS

WESTBOW
PRESS®
A DIVISION OF THOMAS NELSON
& ZONDERVAN

WestBow Press books may be ordered through booksellers or by contacting:

WestBow Press
A Division of Thomas Nelson & Zondervan
1663 Liberty Drive
Bloomington, IN 47403
www.westbowpress.com
1 (866) 928-1240

ISBN: 978-1-9736-6785-8 (sc)
ISBN: 978-1-9736-6786-5 (e)

Library of Congress Control Number: 2019909262

Print information available on the last page.

WestBow Press rev. date: 7/16/2019

I DEDICATE THIS BOOK TO ALL THE BROKEN WHO HAVE EXPERIENCED abuse, whether it be physical, emotional, or sexual. It is my prayer that you will find resolve as you read these pages. Some of the things that I relate may never compare to what readers have experienced in their personal lives. There is always more to every story, and I know that there are countless who have experienced far worse than I have in their lives.

We have a tendency to focus on what has occurred in our lives. My prayer is that the focus will be on Jesus Christ. I also pray that you will see the faithfulness of God in my life and how He used the crumpled life of a little girl and showed her His mighty love, grace, and healing.

My hope is that you will read this booklet from my perspective, one that seeks to honor and adore our Lord and Savior. All that He has taken me through in my life are things that formed me into the woman I am, but more important the woman I became in Jesus Christ.

My prayer is that this booklet will be found in healing of mind, soul, and body. I hope it will be a new beginning and restoration will be found in Jesus Christ.

These shadows and shades molded my life, distorted my thinking, and colored my world. But when Jesus Christ came into my life, He became the brilliance that diffused the darkness of my soul. These pages recount a journey of anger and pain into His amazing love and grace.

Acknowledgments

I WOULD LIKE TO EXPRESS MY GREAT APPRECIATION TO ALL WHO have challenged me from past to present to write this booklet. There are many who worked together, family and friends who have proofread and given direction and guidance to me in the preparation of this book. I want to thank you for helping me and inspiring me to go on to present my story and to relate how Jesus Christ rescued me and planted me on a firm foundation.

I am blessed beyond measure by your friendship, your talents, your gifts, and your prayers in the preparation of this book. Thank you.

The Shadows

A VERSE VERY DEAR TO MY HEART IS PSALM 23:4 (AMP), WHICH SAYS, "Yes, though I walk through the [deep, sunless] valley of the shadow of death, I will fear or dread no evil, for You are with me; Your rod [to protect] and Your staff [to guide], they comfort me." That tells, in part, about the beginnings of my shadows.

Just what is a shadow? It can be an illusion, an emptiness of all sorts, and a hollowness. It can be blackness. It is an image cast upon light, a dark replica of something. There are the recollections of my shadows.

I was born into a predominately Russian German home. My mother's parents fled to American in 1906 from Russia during the Russo-Japanese War. My grandfather became a citizen of the United States in 1937. He was a farmer and a carpenter who made beautifully carved furniture. My grandmother was a homemaker. They had eleven children; my mom was the tenth child. My grandparents celebrated seventy years of married life together.

My dad's parents were German French. Grandpa Joseph was from southeast Nebraska, as was Grandma Mary. Grandpa was a farmer, and Grandma was a homemaker. They had two sons, my uncle and my dad.

My dad's dad was a hard man. I honestly did not know him, even though we lived only seven miles apart. He was not a loving grandfather to us.

My dad's mom was a beautiful woman. She was very talented musically and had a strong love for the Lord. She came from a family of nine. She had six brothers. Her dad was a Catholic and was a farmer. After he came to know the Lord personally as his Savior, he preached in the Methodist church for fifty years.

Grandma Mary felt she was overly protected, and she wanted to experience life on the wild side. It was during this rebellious stage that she met my grandpa. He was on the wild side. Even though her parents disapproved of Grandpa, she pursued the relationship, and when she married Grandpa, her parents did not attend the wedding. It broke her heart as well as theirs, but her parents continued to pray that she would return to her Lord and Savior.

Their prayers were answered. When Grandma came back to the Lord, she came back! She gave up all the things they used to do together. She went to church and rededicated her life to Christ. Her desires and Grandpa's desires were now direct opposites. She refused to go with Grandpa to places that were against her Christian values, and they had a very distant relationship in their marriage. She paid the price for her rebellious nature against her parents' counsel and God's design. I know a little about that price, but she made a choice to continue to live with Grandpa.

ELAINE LEWIS

She still managed to become a lovely person in spite of Grandpa's treatment of her.

Grandpa's treatment never stopped my grandmother from praying for him. I remember her gathering my brother and me around a hassock to pray that Grandpa would be saved. He walked in, heard us praying for him, and was outraged.

After her death, I was grieving deeply when she came to me in a vision with a message for Grandpa. She wanted me to tell him that she forgave him and loved him, and she wanted him to join her in heaven.

Grandpa voiced his regret about his treatment of Grandma. He wondered if she could ever forgive him, so I shared Grandma's special message to him: she had forgiven him. I believe, in part, that that message led to his salvation on his deathbed.

There was a definite difference in the way Grandma and Grandpa treated my brother and me compared to our cousins. Grandpa showered his attention upon my uncle's children. We never knew any love from Grandpa, but Grandma always extended her arms to both us and our cousins. She loved them as much as she loved us.

Grandma Mary taught my brother and me how to play the piano, and we would sing choruses. What beautiful memories I have of her. She became a confidante to me as I grew older, and I knew she would love me no matter what. She enjoyed having fun, and oh, my, I loved to hear her laugh. She was a fun-loving grandmother who had an intense desire to serve the Lord. What an impact she had on me. Thank you, Grandma, for your love. You made a godly imprint on my life.

My dad was quite an athlete in his day. He loved to play baseball. He played first base in the local leagues and was almost recruited to the White Sox. However, he was drafted into the

US Marine Corps during World War II. Dad always felt like life cheated him from playing in the big leagues because the opportunity to play professional ball never came again.

After the war, Dad came back to our southwest town in Nebraska and began farming with his dad. Shortly after that, he met and married my mother, who was five years his senior. Mom was a real beauty and was a waitress and a bookkeeper. Both Dad and Mom were perfectionists. Dad raised wheat and cattle on our farm. Mom was a homemaker.

I was born in January. In those days, the winters were harsh. The day I was born, my dad was so disappointed I was a girl that he left my mom and me alone in the hospital for four days, and no one knew where he went. (I was told this by my grandmother and will address this in a later chapter.)

My earliest recollections of life came when I was hurled over a tall fence into my grandmother's arms. A few days later, at eighteen months of age, I was introduced to my brother.

Our home was not happy. Dad was always angry, and Mom ... well, she just tried to keep the peace. None of us ever really knew what would set Dad off or what he would do to any of us. Consequently, we all walked on eggshells around him.

Many unhappy incidents ring out in my mind, but one stands out. One morning Mom had prepared eggs for my dad. Dad liked his eggs either scrambled or hard. On this morning, he picked up his plate and threw it up against the wall. We watched in horror as the contents slid down the wall. Mom cried, and we cried right along with her. I remember his eyes were full of fury. We all knew we must tiptoe around him or there would be a price to pay.

For me today, mealtimes are among the most significant gatherings we have as a family. We get to gather around the

ELAINE LEWIS

table, laugh, share our work stories, or plan the next day's events. It is also a time to pray and have a cup of coffee with a dear friend. It is a special time to play games, to make snakes with Play-Doh, to do crafts, or to make noodles and cookies. Our table is used in beautiful ways to be with family and friends.

What a joy to live on the farm. We grew up loving the animals because there was not much love in our home. We always had an abundance of kittens and puppies to play with and love, but at times it seemed like a curse. At a very young age, I had to put those precious little kittens and puppies in a gunnysack and drown them while Dad held my hand down in the water. I cried and begged him not to make me do this, but he would not relent. On many occasions, I was forced to watch him throw these little animals against the shed as tears streamed down my face. I wondered, *If Dad can do this to puppies and kittens, what can he do to me?*

From what I have been told, I was a spunky child. In other words, I was strong-willed! I would go out to the yard, and if Mom came out to check on me, I would hide behind a tree. It was like playing hide-and-seek, and Mom was it! She would grow frantic as she called to me, but I would be as quiet as a mouse. Many times she found me enjoying the game despite her frustration.

I do not know for sure how old I was when I decided to walk out to the field where my dad was disking the ground. He was about a mile away from the house. At that time, we had a big, white German shepherd whose name I don't remember. He went with me everywhere and was my faithful friend and guardian. On this fateful day, he and I headed across the fallowed ground on an adventure. We saw all kinds of things on our walk, including little birds trying to find their overturned nests in the tilled soil, all sorts of bugs, and field mice scampering to find safety as we merrily walked along.

Back at the house, Mom desperately called me but could not find me anywhere. I am sure she was looking behind those trees! Mom looked up and saw a little figure with a big white dog heading to meet my dad on the tractor about half a mile away. She gathered my brother up in her arms and started to run after me. My dad must have seen me at the same time. By the time Mom reached me, my dad had too. He was furious at me and Mom for this little adventure. Dad scolded me and raised his hand to spank me, but the big, white dog grabbed my dad's arm and pulled him to the ground, growling at him. I did not get a spanking that day.

The next day, I could not find my dog. I called and called for him. He always came to greet me as soon as I stepped one little foot outside the door, but not this day. I began to cry. Where was he?

Later in the day, Dad said he had found my white dog. He took me to the borrow pit, where my beautiful white dog lay dead. Dad told me that he had been run over by a car. I lost my friend and protector that day.

Several years later, I learned that the big, white dog did not die by a car but by my dad's hand. Dad had shot him because the dog had tried to protect me from Dad's anger. I understand in part why Dad did that, but within me, an awful emotion began to grow. It was called anger, and I started to mistrust my dad and his actions.

Dad seemed to enjoy hurting those who were weaker than he was. He would laugh and make fun of me if I shed tears over a drama I watched on TV. I still cry today when I see sad stories. He tried to squelch any tenderness or love I showed to animals or people. It was not okay to feel or express emotions. I was oppressed.

Dad was a selfish man. We could only do the things *he* wanted to do, watch programs *he* wanted to watch, or go places *he* wanted to go. None of us had a choice. We had to do what he wanted, or a price would have to be paid.

One year we put up a grain bin, and it was pretty tall. I remember my brother and I had to get up on ladders and put the nuts on the bolts. I was close to the top rung of the ladder. Dad was down on the floor of the bin. I leaned over to put a nut on the bolt when Dad began to shake the ladder. I begged him to stop, but he would not. I started to cry as I held on for dear life. He almost bounced me off the ladder. I was terrified partly of the height but more by what I saw in Dad's eyes.

Shadows of mistrust and fear formed. Many questions loomed in my mind, but the question above all others was, "Why does Dad seem to hate me?" He was not to be trusted. I had no answers to my questions.

The rural community in which I grew up was sexually charged. We saw it in the country school with the kids and their parents, and later in high school and in our town. No matter where we went, there was sexual interaction between the younger kids and older kids, between parents and children. Some husbands and wives even swapped spouses.

There were many situations where kids in our country school exploited each other during sleepovers. I was exposed to it in many ways, as were all the other kids. I know of two incidents when things got out of hand, and it was brought to the attention of a parent, but nothing was ever done about it.

Many times I would sit by my mom when my folks visited

other couples in our country school. She would literally push me away from her and "threaten" me with her eyes to "go play." However, I did not want to leave because I knew what would happen to me. I told her twice about certain exploitations, but she thought I was lying, and no action was ever taken. She admonished me for telling lies about those "nice kids." Instead, many shadows began to molest me. Many people knew things, but nothing was ever done, so the victimization continued.

One day, as we were traveling in the truck to the cattle sale, Dad asked me to get a book out the cubbyhole for him. I reached in and took it out. He then asked me to open it up. I was conditioned to do just as he said. When I opened it, I saw all kinds of bad things that little girls should never see. I looked at Dad, ashamed and embarrassed. He saw my embarrassment and shame, and he tried to make it my fault for getting the book out in the first place. What I saw was pornography. Why would a father allow his little girl to see such images? I was never asked again to go with him to the cattle sales, and I no longer felt special. Feeling special was now a shadow, like a phantom that appears and disappears.

There was one other incident like the first one, and it bears the same truth. I was fifteen. Dad always liked his vehicles cleaned inside and out. On this day, he specifically asked me to clean out underneath the seats of the pickup. While I was doing this, I found some magazines. With interest, I pulled them out and began to look at them. I was sitting so engrossed in what I was viewing that I did not hear my dad walk up. He asked me what I was doing. I was immediately ashamed and tried to hide the magazines, but I had been caught. He then accused me of buying these magazines in town when I drove to school with my learner's permit. I denied it over and over, but he condemned me on the spot. "I did not do this," I told him. He told me to burn the magazines, which I did. I was a good, obedient child who had to obey an angry father. In the wake of this incident, I was left with conflicting emotions. Why did he do this? Why was it always my fault? I was not guilty of this!

Some of my aunts and uncles took an interest in me as a child and teenager. I don't exactly know why because it seemed to me that I was the most unlovable person in the world. I would crawl up on my aunt's lap, and she would love me to death.

One day after high school, I stopped at my special uncle and aunt's house. I think my aunt was having a guilty memory moment. She wanted to make restitution and asked if I would forgive them for what they did to me as a child. I could not begin to imagine what that could be. She told me that before my parents became Christians, they all would have drinking parties. Many of them were held in our home because Mom and Dad had two little kids. She told me that they used to get me drunk and watch me hit furniture and tumble all around. They thought it was hilarious; I was their entertainment for the night. Anger burned inside me when I heard that. I could not believe that my family could do something so horrible at the expense of a child. Who were these people? Once again I felt worthless, unloved, and not cherished. At that very moment, I began to hate my parents intensely.

I went home and confronted my mom about what my aunt had said. Mom said it was right, and she wondered why my aunt would tell me this now. "Obviously, she knew she was guilty and needed forgiveness," I said. I forgave my aunt and uncle eventually, but the pain inside was great. To be used and abused in that way was horrific for me. I felt abandoned and rejected. I never once heard my mother say she was sorry or regretted her actions toward me, her child. My anger grew. A shadow of blackness came over my soul.

During our childhood, Dad was always in the pool hall, a place where one gambled and drank alcohol; we would call it a bar today. My aunt and uncle lived in an apartment next door to the pool hall that Dad frequented most of the time.

On one occasion, while visiting my aunt and uncle, Dad went to the pool hall. It was getting late, and Mom asked me to slip down into the pool hall, find my dad, and tell him that Mom was ready to go home.

As I approached the doorway, I encountered many pungent scents. The smell of alcohol along with cigarette smoke filled the small room. It was very dark and dimly lit. The jukebox was playing, and in the dark I could hear my dad talking and laughing. I did not call out to him; I knew better than that. I crept behind the bar on my hands and knees. I heard no voices except my dad's voice and a woman's voice. When I got to the end of the bar, I peeked around and saw my dad and a woman passionately kissing each other. I had never seen any affection like this displayed between my parents. I did not know how to process the visual before me. I was hit with a flood of emotions, including anger.

I turned around and crawled the length of the bar on my hands and knees. Then I slipped out amid darkness and smoke. My thoughts filled with many questions. If I told my mom what I saw, would it wreck our home? Why did Dad not love Mom? Why was he kissing that woman? What should I tell Mom? I did not know what to do.

As I approached the long steps to the apartment, I sat down and cried. I was so overwhelmed. What should I share with Mom? My little steps were heavy. I felt like I had bricks in my shoes as I made the long trek up the steep stairs. I dried my tears with my shirt and went into the apartment. Mom asked me if I had seen Dad, and I said, "Yes, he will be coming soon." I had just participated in his lies.

After I got my driver's license, I followed my dad to see if he was really going where he said he was going. I would make up some excuse, a lie, to Mom that I needed something for a school project. I would then follow him. He drove to a town about eighteen miles away from our home. He always went to the same house. In fact, I could take you to it today. He was greeted with a kiss by the woman who lived there. I would park in an obscure place and wait until he came out a few hours later. As soon as I saw him leave, I would take the country roads home so I would arrive home before he got there. He never knew I knew. My anger boiled inside of me. I grew to hate him and everything he did or did not do. He said he was a Christian, but I never believed him based on his behavior.

There are many things I could share on these pages—so much more—but I think you get the picture of what events shaped my life. All these examples were but precursors of what changed my life, my outlook, my spontaneity, my trust, and how I looked through rose-colored glasses then and still do today.

This was a significant shadow. This shadow molded my life in various ways and influenced how I thought, how I processed, how I felt, how I trusted (or didn't trust), how I felt about myself, and how I believed. It was ever before me while growing up, but I did not know its full impact. I locked it away to survive, and it took a cataclysmic event, a key, to unlock the chest.

The Shades

Just what is a shade? It is a variance, a contrast, or a tint of color. My shades were seen as masks or dyes to cover up the pain I sometimes experienced daily.

I remember school days. When I first entered kindergarten, I was just five years old and very fearful. I was afraid of the teacher and the other kids in our little country school. I was very timid. Not too many days into my new school experience, I made a statement that my dad had shot a rabbit. The kids laughed at the way I said the word *rabbit*. I thought they were making fun of me. After that, I would not say another word in that one-room schoolhouse. No matter how hard my teacher tried to get me to speak, I would not. She would have to send all the other kids out to recess first before I would talk to her. She would teach me during recess, but as soon as the big kids came in, I was as silent as a mouse. As I look back, I see it made her teaching very difficult, but I adored her. She told my mom that I was a super sensitive kid.

I had her until about fifth grade. We had several teachers after her who were not very helpful. One teacher made fun of me because I could not understand math, and I would have to stay inside and work the problems until I could get them. I never got recesses. She made me cry when I asked for help. Then she would make fun of me when I did not understand something. I hated school. Country school was never the same after my first special teacher.

No matter where I was, at home or in school, I lived under a shade of worthlessness. I had to adapt to my surroundings. Like a chameleon, I chose to blend in to hide all the rejection I felt. It was not okay to be angry in my world, so I developed attitudes that had different shades and tints to adjust to any situation.

I was always striving to be better than my brother. It seemed that whatever he put his hand to, he did it well. He was good in school. He was on honor roll. He had natural abilities in sports and music, and he had the blessing of my parents. No matter what I seemed to do, it was always inferior to my brother.

Grade school and high school were no different. I was always compared to my brother. His grades and the blessings he received from teachers were exceptional. I was always asked by our teachers, "Why aren't you like your brother? He is so smart and talented!" In other words, I was dumb!

At parent-teacher conferences, my folks told me how the teachers were so proud of my brother and his achievements, but they never had anything positive to say about me. I felt like a zero.

There were two times in my life when my anger got the best of me. One time was in high school during home economics class. I don't remember all the specific details, but I had just been teased and made fun of, so I was already angry when I walked into the classroom. I had a chip on my shoulder. I was defiant, and nobody was going to tell me what to do. Just before entering the class, I stuck a piece of gum in my mouth and chewed it vigorously. (In my day, you could not chew gum anywhere in the school.) I sat down at my desk, and my teacher asked me if I was chewing gum. I defiantly said, "Yes, I am." She asked me to take it out. Anger instantaneously gripped me. In defiance, I said to her, "If you want it, come get it yourself!" She made a move toward me, and I lost it. I began to throw chairs around the classroom and was out of control. My teacher and my classmates were shocked at my display of anger.

The principal was called, and he ushered me to his office. He sat me down and asked me why I had exploded in anger. I told him I did not know why I had reacted this way. He told me that I had always been an obedient student who obeyed the rules. He was baffled by my actions. I was too.

He told me that the punishment for such behavior was suspension from school for a few days. He was going to call my parents. At that moment, I determined I would run away from home. I would not bear the abuse any longer. Whatever showed in my eyes changed his mind. He said he would not kick me out of school or call my parents, but if I ever acted this way again, I would be expelled from school. That day, the principal showed me mercy and grace.

The second incident is much closer to my heart. It was a defining moment for me, and I am ashamed to tell you about it now, but I hope it will help you to understand the power and effect of words upon our lives. It shows anger in its most deadly form.

My brother was drying the dishes, and I was washing them. He began to tease me and make fun of my body. I asked him to quit, but he pressed on. I again asked him to stop, but he was on a roll; it seemed he could not stop teasing me. My anger rose. In the sink, filled with soapy water, was a big butcher knife waiting to be washed. I picked it up, and in an instant I slammed my brother against the kitchen cabinets with the knife in hand, ready to strike. As quickly as I slammed him against the cabinets, I realized this was my brother, whom I loved. I threw the knife down, ran to my secret hiding place, and wept with gut-wrenching sobs. At that moment, I promised my anger would never control me again, and it never has—at least, to that degree. My brother never teased me in that way ever again.

As I mentioned before, both of our parents were perfectionists. All chores or jobs had to be done correctly and accurately— no exceptions. Mom found her outlet in cleaning. She always cleaned. I am sure it was her escape from all that faced in our home. She was relentless when we cleaned. She would give me the bathroom to clean, and if it did not meet her standard of perfection, she would scold me and do it herself all over again. I never wanted to be in the house because I could never do anything well enough to please her. I found my outlet outdoors.

At one stage of their lives, my parents raised chickens. They had bought them as chicks and used them for laying eggs. They sold the eggs to the poultry store. The eggs were gathered and taken down to the basement, where they had to be washed, put in egg cartons, packed, and stacked to sell.

One day, my brother and I decided to go downstairs to play. While there, I had an idea to throw the eggs in the buckets against the wall. My brother was reluctant to do this, but I encouraged him by throwing the first egg at the wall. We had thrown most of the eggs when we heard our mother's voice. She asked what we were doing. I replied for the two of us and said, "Nothing, Mom." She said she was coming down to check on us. Immediately, we felt like Adam and Eve in the garden; we knew we were in trouble, and we had better hide.

There was an old iron bed and some other furniture in the corner of the basement, so we made a mad dash and slid under the old bed where Mom couldn't get to us because it was too heavy for her to move.

Now, as a mom myself, I can only imagine the frustration when she saw the destruction of her basement. She was absolutely outraged at what we had done. She yelled for us to come out, but we did not. She tried to move the old iron bed to get to us, but she could not. She yelled and screamed at us, but we stayed quiet and still. (You could bet if my kids did that, I would have tanned their hides and made them do the cleanup. No bed would have stopped my fury!) Finally, her cleaning obsession kicked in, and she started cleaning up our mess. It took her a few hours to clean it up. We watched her from under the bed. As I write this now, my heart aches for her and her great exasperation. She was utterly exhausted from her labors.

She said nothing to us as she went upstairs. My heart hurt for her because of our act of disobedience and our fun at her expense. My brother and I went out the backdoor. We never did get a spanking for this incident, but we never did it again. She didn't tell Dad what we had done, and I don't know how she explained the loss of the eggs to him. If she had told him, there would have been a price to pay.

There were only a couple of times in my youth where I remember my mom really laughing. She was so solemn and self-controlled, and she always walked on eggshells to please my dad.

One afternoon, she asked me if I wanted to walk with her up to the field, which was about a mile away. As we walked together, something tickled her, and she laughed and giggled all the way to the meadow and back. On another occasion, when she was getting ready for a bath, she put her toes under the water and got such a kick out of that; she giggled and giggled. It is funny what we remember from being kids.

Dad and Mom lived a persona of always looking good no matter what. To me, they looked like Mr. and Mrs. Jekyll and Hyde. On the outside to people, friends, and family, they looked good, but in our home we all knew the truth.

I remember the countless times when Dad played with our cousins in ways he never played with us. He threw them up in the air or swung them round and round. If we got in line for him to play with us, he always pushed us aside and shamed us for asking for the same treatment. My brother and I were often jealous of the interaction and attention our cousins received from our dad. They thought that he was the greatest uncle ever. He may have been to them, but we always wondered why our cousins were so special and his own kids were not.

No one really knew what went on behind closed doors in our home. In the rural community and at church, my dad was well liked and respected, but at home he was a different person. Mom's job was to keep peace at all costs. Even if something was not her fault, she would make apologies to mend the rift she felt among us all. As we grew older and more rebellious, she would always make the first move to patch the differences between us. Mom danced to Dad's tune most of her married life.

Mom was a great Sunday school teacher to the adults at the church where we attended. Most of her pastors revered her insights into God's Word. For years now, many of her peers have told me what a great teacher she was. In this arena, she was able to come out from under the cloak that hid and bound her in our home. This was where she found her gift and fulfillment.

I never felt like our parents ever really wanted us. In fact, I was pretty sure I was adopted or that a switch had been made. It seemed like my parents hated me.

Hope was of little consequence to me as a child in our home, but now I see how hope carried me through some of the most challenging times in my life. It was there; I simply did not see it as clearly as I see it now. "For You have been a stronghold for the poor, a stronghold for the needy in his distress, a shelter from the storm, a shade from the heat; for the blast of the ruthless ones is like a rainstorm against the wall" (Isaiah 25:4 AMP).

ELAINE LEWIS

Saturation

<small>WHAT IS THE DEFINITION OF SATURATION?</small> *MERRIAM-WEBSTER'S* defines it as being completely soaked or absorbed.

While growing up, I had many raging emotions. I saw that my mother had a more profound faith than my father. Though Dad talked a strong faith, he never walked it. To others he was a great man, but to me he was a rascal!

I was confused about how to live my life and how to be a Christian. I did not want to be like my dad, living a double life. I took the role of protector to my mom. I felt sorry for her and at the same time felt ambivalence toward her. Those were such conflicting emotions. I often wondered if she really knew my father, her husband. I knew him, and I hated him.

By the time I got out on my own, I was thoroughly convinced I was a complete idiot and there was nothing good about me. On the outside, I played the game just like my parents. I led a double life.

To others, I appeared as kind, caring, and a loyal friend. I was even homecoming queen in high school and was the first runner-up in college. How could that be? I was nothing, or so I believed.

I lived to meet the expectations of others. What a vicious cycle it was. If I did not feel accepted or if I failed in any way, I changed my life to please those around me. I became a chameleon, just like my dad. I was hurting inside but pretending on the outside that all was okay. I lived in my own personal hell. There was no joy, only pressure to maintain the façade. I was often told I would never measure up, and I was a great disappointment to my parents. I regretted my existence.

I soaked up all the emotions that ran rampant in our family. I caught each one of them.

When Mom could not deal with Dad's many moods, she would send me out to calm him. I did so cautiously because I was an obedient child. I would test the waters to make sure that the backlash would not hurt too much. If I told a joke and he laughed, I knew that his mood would soften. If I did not achieve success in breaking his attitude, I would leave him alone. I was successful most of the time. When I succeeded, this brought praise from Mom. Through the years, I learned to watch eyes and to take note of what I saw in them. This allowed me to gauge the reactions I saw and then engage or step away.

How we treat animals of any kind will determine how they react to us. Even chickens gauge emotions. As much as I loved animals, I hated chickens. One old rooster took in our feelings and responded to them. My brother and I used to ride our bikes through flocks of chickens, and many times one would get caught in the spokes of our bikes, and the rider would fall. It was fun. We would take sticks and hit the chickens and the old rooster. We would tease the old rooster in various ways. The old rooster took all of our antics in, and his bird brain saw us to be a threat to him and his hens. He did not back down. He became braver and would start to chase us whether we were on foot or riding our bikes. Of course, we would never stand our ground. We ourselves became chickens, and we ran!

One crisp spring day, I leisurely walked across the yard with no intent of harassing the chickens or the rooster. Out of the corner of my eye, I saw the old rooster running toward me. He was on the prowl, and I was the prey! I started running, and so did he. Though his wings were clipped, he took flight and landed on my shoulders. I turned around and ran back to the house. The old bird was having his day. He dug his claws into my shoulders and began pecking my head. What a sight that must have been. I could hear his wings flapping in the air behind me. I reached my dad, who wore a smile on his face that said to me, "You finally got what you deserved." Dad took the old rooster off my shoulders and wrung his neck. We ate him that night for supper—and by the way, he did not go down well.

The old rooster taught me that what we do to others comes back to us in some way. It was the pecking order in many ways. We were hurt, and after we were saturated, we took it out on others. The old rooster had enough of our abuse, and he was driven by his hate for us. He defended himself and his hens from two kids who had been saturated by their own anger. At that moment, we were no different than our father.

My brother and I loved to shoot our BB guns at anything. We shot birds and rabbits, and we shot windows out of the shop. On one occasion we were shooting around the chicken house even though Dad had explicitly said to not go around the chickens because it would scare them and prevent them from laying their eggs. But Dad had gone to town and said he wouldn't be back until later. We watched him drive out of the yard, and then I said to my brother, "Let's go in the chicken house and shoot birds." My brother was reluctant because of Dad's warning, but I convinced him to come along anyway. I reasoned we could do it before Dad got back, and he would never know. We were shooting when I noticed Dad driving back into the yard. We were caught. How would we get out of the chicken coop without him seeing us with our guns? We did not think of simply leaving them in the chicken shed. Instead, we walked out with guns in our hands. We inched slowly out. He saw us and asked if we had been shooting in there. I replied no, but my brother said yes. Busted! Of course, I got the spanking because my brother had told the truth.

As I said, I hated chickens, and they were my focal point. One time Dad asked if I had turned on the air compressor in the shop. I said, "No, I didn't, but maybe a chicken turned it on by walking over it." I was spanked for saying that. I was always in trouble. It had seemed like a reasonable explanation because the chickens were everywhere. I lied a lot. Lying was my only defense. I was told I was a naughty girl. Ironically, this time I was not lying because I did not know how to turn on an air compressor.

Beatings were hard. I can remember getting spanked with a willow branch, and I was unable to sit or lie down for a few days without significant pain. My brother would always cry before he got a spanking, so he rarely got one. Defiance was my name. I was a strong-willed child in many ways, but I was broken on the inside. I was saturated with confusing emotions, but I used my mask well, and no one knew how I felt. I did not even understand my own feelings.

I always worried about whether I chose the right thing to do. Choices were hard to make because I worried what the outcome might be. My insecurity kept me from taking initiative and stepping out. No matter what I chose, it always seemed to be the wrong decision, so to be on the safe side, I held back.

I had so many questions as to who I was. I did not know, but Jesus knew all about me from the beginning. He told me I was His. It was not who I thought I was, but it was He who calmed the storms in me.

My brother was an exceptional athlete and student. My heart ached for him in the area of sports. Dad was a great athlete, and he expected no less of my brother. My brother did not want to go out for football, but Dad insisted and shamed him until he did. The first day of practice, my brother was hit on the side of the knee and had to have major surgery. It put him out of football for the year. He had to have multiple surgeries on his knees because Dad wanted him to shine as he had in his youth.

After his surgery, my brother had to wear a knee brace. He enjoyed playing basketball, but it could not have been much fun for him because after every game, we had to sit around the table and discuss what my brother did or did not do in the game. My brother always ended up crying because Dad put pressure on him to play better. When he played, he was afraid to make a mistake on the court because he knew what was waiting for him after the game. When he cried, I cried along with him. He was never praised for the good plays he made or for the points he made; instead, the negative was always emphasized. It was a hard time. Dad often told him what a disappointment he was on the basketball court and how he could have played the game better.

Dad was so disappointed in my brother's basketball abilities that he told me he wished I could play because I was better than my brother. I even had a PE coach tell my dad that he wished that I had been a boy because I had athletic ability. Who was I?

We had a little Ford tractor, which we used to check our cows about two miles away. (We did not have ATVs in our day.) Dad told me to take the tractor and check the cows. It was awesome because I could leave and do my own thing. I got to the gate, jumped off the tractor, and opened the gate. As I turned around to get back on the tractor, I saw it bouncing down the hill. My first thought was that Dad was going to kill me. What an idiot I was. I ran after the tractor thinking I could stop it or jump on it like a cowboy bringing down a calf. It reached the bottom of the hill, and I was right behind it. As it bounced down those hills, the key jiggled out. Now what would I do? Those two miles were tough to walk. I knew Dad would explode. This was just another dumb thing to add to my list of stupid mistakes.

Dad was working steers when I got home. I slowly inched my way over to him, and he saw I had been crying. He asked what was wrong, so I told him. I was waiting for "Old Faithful" to blow when he got a sheepish grin on his face and told me not to worry; he had done the same thing once before. We both had left it in neutral instead of shutting it off and putting it in gear. It was the first time I had ever heard my dad admit he had made a mistake. I was about sixteen years old.

My name was Trouble. No matter where I went or what I did, I was always in trouble. My appearance, what I wore, what I ate, and how I acted in the home and outside of the house were continuously scrutinized. Perfect behavior was expected in public and at church. I could never be a kid. I could never have fun. I did not know who I was. I was a prototype of my parents. We were always told that a good name was everything, and if I messed up or that good name came into question, I would bring dishonor and shame to them. For fifty-three years of my life, I never heard "I am proud of you" or "I love you." I knew I was hated, but I did not know why.

As I stated earlier, my Dad's mom, my grandmother, was a special person in my life. I would tell her all of my thoughts and feelings. I was about fifteen when I asked her why Dad seemed to hate me so much. She struggled, trying to avoid answering my question. I pressed her and would not let her off the hook. She finally told me that on the day of my birth, Dad was so disappointed that I was not a boy, he'd left Mom and me in the hospital for four days, and no one knew where he had gone. This answer might seem malicious coming from a grandmother, but she was being pressed by a perplexed young girl who was not going to give up until she had answers to her question. She told me Dad did love me, but it was hard for him to express it in a way I'd understand. My anger continued to burn deep inside of me, and the seeds of hate and doubt drank in more of the same. My grandmother attempted to minimize my feelings of rejection, but it instead maximized my hatred and my feelings of worthlessness.

Yet many celebrated my existence. My grandmother, two pastors' wives, and two special aunts poured love into me when my parents did not. They were a link, a chain to hold on to. They filled my heart tank and positively shaped my life. I praise God for their love and willingness to care for me. They were beacons of light to a little girl and teenager who was drifting on the dark seas of despair. I think in some marvelous way, all those special women knew I needed their attention. I think they sensed I felt abandoned and rejected. What they offered me were love and acceptance, and I freely drank from that well of love and acceptance. This was enough to sustain me through the rough times of false expectation and impending doom. I have often wondered why I did not take a different path; I sure could have. It would have been justifiable given the circumstances of my life, but we all have choices to make. I did make some wrong decisions based upon my perceptions rather than what was right. Yet through it all, God protected me. His eye was upon me even though I was not choosing Him!

Proverbs 15:3 (AMP) states, "The eyes of the Lord are in every place, keeping watch upon the evil and the good." No matter what place I was in, He was watching. His eyes were upon me. This verse continues to offer great hope to me in other situations and circumstances.

The History

M<small>Y BEST FRIEND FROM HIGH SCHOOL AND</small> I <small>DECIDED TO GO TO</small> airline school after graduation. We attended airline school and then graduated. I had the opportunity at an airport in Chicago. I was offered the job, but I was too timid and insecure to take it. I was not sure what to do for my life's work.

My brother had just graduated from high school, and he was planning on attending a Christian university in Denver. He wanted to know if I wanted to attend with him. I checked it out and completed my paperwork, and off we went to college. My brother left after his first year there to pursue a career in electronics. I stayed on at the university for two more years. It was there that I dedicated my life to Jesus Christ as my Lord and Savior. Why? Because I was blinded by my hurt and anger, and I felt distressed and abandoned. When Jesus came, He changed everything for me. He filled my life with gladness and gave me purpose and identity.

I wanted a change, so I left college. I heard that there was a Christian organization in eastern Nebraska that was hiring typists. I applied and was appointed to work in the legal department.

My four years there enabled me to develop skills I could use for future employment. I learned office skills such as typing, dictation, and using a Dictaphone. These were essential skills for a receptionist. Working there gave me incredible knowledge and experience about how to work with people, how to interact with others and situations, and how to live life. It was a springboard for me into life's experiences.

While working there, one of my principal supervisors challenged me and gave me courage to examine many areas of my life that were confusing. She questioned me regarding legalism and my beliefs about doctrinal issues. She gave me great devotionals from God's Word, many of which I still remember to this day. I became involved in in-depth Bible studies. It was an excellent learning and growing experience in my walk with the Lord. I praise God for the many who inspired me to live wholly for Him.

I experienced many life lessons while living and working there. I worked with difficult people who reminded me of my upbringing. There was another supervisor in my office who despised me as my dad had. I never knew why she did not like me, but I felt that my time there was coming to an end.

I remember looking through the classified ads in the paper and seeing a posting for a police dispatcher in western Nebraska. The job sounded exciting and intriguing to me. I applied for the job and took the test. Even though I had not heard whether the job was mine, I gave my notice at work and moved home. Fearful, insecure me had made a bold decision. Somehow, I knew I had the job.

My parents were not happy that I had quit my employment without knowing I had a job in western Nebraska. (Yes, I do not recommend that either, but I just knew the job was mine.) My folks told me how stupid I had been for quitting my job. I should have waited to give my two weeks' notice until I knew for sure. I began to have doubts. Then I received the call from the police department telling me the job was mine. They asked me to start in two weeks.

While employed at the police department, I decided to look up some old friends who had attended my university. They lived in the same area as I did now. I learned that their dad was the pastor of one of the local churches in town. I attended a service and reacquainted myself with my future husband. We were good friends in college, and he was now farming with his father. We were married a year later. He was the first male who showed me what unconditional love was. I had never experienced love, let alone unconditional love, until I married my husband. He was a gift from God!

Nineteen months later, a son was born to us, and sixteen months later, a little girl entered our home. Then two years later, another son joined our family. Each child brought a different dimension to our lives.

Our oldest son was always the cautious one. He seemed to sense my needs, and he has a caring, sensitive heart. Our daughter always tested the limits. She loved to upset the apple cart in all of our lives. She has a tender, warm heart with a beautiful smile. Our youngest is a very discerning young man who has a heart of compassion. Each child was gifted and showed strong leadership abilities.

Our daughter's life was changed in junior high. We were never sure exactly what caused this change, but she was no longer the daughter we knew. She ran away from home, and by the time we found out she had skipped school, she had already been on the road for six hours. Later, we found out she had fled to California. We did not know whether we would ever see her again—alive or dead. It was one of the darkest times in our lives.

Exhaustion and worry set in, in a big way. My anxiety, loss, and grief were at their highest peak, and I began to dream. My dreams were heavy and black. I woke in a sweat, and I was flooded with what had happened to me in my life, in the shadows. My memories were vivid and came in huge waves. I felt like I was being crushed. I could not breathe and felt like I was being suffocated. Oh, how it hurt! In the midst of black emotions about our daughter, I remembered how my dad had taken advantage of me sexually. I was about six or seven when my Mom rushed me to the doctor to ask if I was okay. I did not understand the terms he had used, and neither do I remember the outcome of that visit.

Shame flooded my being. I remembered. I remembered. Mom knew, Dad knew, and the doctor knew. It dawned on me then that I had not been a virgin on the day I had married my husband. I vomited and could not stop gagging.

Our daughter's running away was paramount in my fears. I struggled with many questions and felt like I was going crazy. I had a family to care for, but it was almost more than I could bear. I wanted to run like my daughter had, far away to a castle and hide so no one could see me. But I could not; I had to stay and maintain. I was drowning, and the waves were tossing me like a mindless ball on the ocean. I felt like I was dying—in fact, I wanted to die. I contemplated death. I was in quicksand, and it was devouring me. In all honesty, I genuinely don't know how I survived, except for God.

I thank God for His provision of a song or a verse that

ELAINE LEWIS

would come in the night to me. I read the Psalms where David acknowledges his sin with Bathsheba: "I am weary with my groaning; all night I soak my pillow with tears. I drench my couch with my weeping" (Psalm 6:6 AMP). My heart hurt from the pain. Yes, God gave me a song in the darkest of nights. He never let go of me, and I held tightly to Him.

We found our daughter after she had been in California for two weeks. She came back, but she would not maintain our rules. We let her go live her life immersed in the drug culture. Letting her go was one of the hardest things to do.

Our daughter had a little girl about four years later—our first grandchild. For the first eighteen months of her life, she lived with us. Four years later, another daughter was born to our daughter. Both are beautiful girls, and we praise God for them.

In the meantime, our boys grew up with their own emotions and pain regarding their sister's actions and lifestyle. The boys felt their individual pain as well as the pain we went through as a family. Without a doubt, I know they deeply love their sister.

I believe that situations such as this affect our whole lives inside out. We all were touched in some way because our emotions and experiences were impacted.

Many things can shape our lives in definite ways. We know we made many mistakes in the raising of our children. Many times, we were out of the loop when we should have been in the know. We have asked our kids to forgive us. They saw and experienced our weaknesses and frailties. We were not perfect parents. We did the best we could, and sometimes our best was just not good enough.

Since becoming a grandparent, I have looked back and asked God to mend the fences and patch the holes of all our hearts because we do not want to duplicate these mistakes in our next generation. We all need to love and forgive each other when the time is appropriate, and healing will come. This can only be accomplished through God and His great love and mercy.

In 1999, my dad was diagnosed with ALS (Lou Gehrig's disease), and in 2000, in his living room, he asked me to forgive him for what he'd done to me as a child. I told him that I had already forgiven him. As I had grown in my relationship with Jesus Christ, I knew He was asking me to forgive my dad for his actions against me. It was hard and gut-wrenching to do, but I had to because the hatred was eating me up inside. God replaced my hate with His love and forgiveness. I have never been sorry that Christ prompted me to forgive my dad. It freed me in ways I cannot express. A transformation had obviously taken place within my heart as well as my dad's. I needed to hear him ask for forgiveness, and it was good to make amends. We were strangers. Father and child, had so many wasted years of guilt and shame. I was fifty-four years old when my dad first told me he loved me. Forgiveness changes people from the inside out. Dad died a year later.

Toward the end of her life, my mother struggled with the memories of what had been done to me. She lived with us for four years before we had to place her in a nursing home. While living with us and while at the nursing home, she would wail with sorrow and tears. She could not be consoled until I talked to her calmly. She would often ask, "Are you all right? Did he hurt you?" At that time, she was in a diminished state. I assured her that I was fine, and it would eventually calm her down. It was a pitiful sight to see her have such raging emotions about what my father had done to me. She carried all the pain. She had to survive too, but in the end it all came out. She carried that pain and heartache for ninety-six years.

ELAINE LEWIS

The past has been forgiven on several levels for me, but the memories live on in my heart and mind. I still have triggers that remind me of the past abuses. Sometimes I wish I could have had a different life. I know God was with me in every situation. It was not his plan for sexual abuse because He gave all men free will to make their choices. I am reminded of a verse in Genesis when Cain had evil thoughts about his brother, Abel. This is what God said to him. "Why are you angry? And why has your countenance fallen? If you do well, will not your countenance be lifted up? *And if you do not do well, sin is crouching at the door; and its desire is for you, but you must master it*" (Genesis 4:6–7 AMP; emphasis mine). Cain had a choice. God was able to deliver Cain from his intents, but he chose to follow his own desires, his anger, and his embarrassment, and he did not take God's escape plan! Just like Cain, my dad was selfish and wanted to fulfill his own passions. God always wants to give us a way to escape from those passions. God could have stopped Cain, but He didn't. He could have prevented my Dad too, and the countless others who have engaged in such hurt and pain. He did not because He gives all a choice to do what is right.

There were several times in my experiences where God showed Himself when these things were being done. I would look up or off to the side and see Jesus standing there with tears rolling down his face. Men's deeds are evil. We have Jesus, who is willing to unravel the string that is so knotted up because of evil men's acts.

Throughout the book, music plays an essential part of my life. I am touched by the words of songs and how God used them to help me through the shadows and shades of abuse. He revealed to me His brilliant light to infuse my journey and give me hope so I can go on.

We all need to know how much we are loved, as well as how God desires to take our hands and lead us through the dark times of our lives. We have scars and wear masks to hide our ugliness, but Jesus's love for us goes deeper than our scars because He died for us and bore the scars for us.

We are reminded of our memories, which can take us low. We do need to be reminded at times as to where we came from and where we are now, in Christ. We don't deserve God's love, but He chose to save us from our sins. It is hard to understand why He loves us so.

We all have memories, some good and some ugly, but no matter what they are, God is with us in them.

It does not mean that we will not experience trials and troubles as we walk in His path, but I do know that He will prevail with us in His brilliant light.

> For once you were darkness, but now you are light in the Lord; walk as children of Light [lead the lives of those native born to the Light]. (Ephesians 5:8 AMP)

Dispersion of Light

WHEN THERE IS A SEPARATION OF VISIBLE LIGHT INTO ITS DIFFERENT colors, it is known as dispersion. The dispersion of light is the basis for understanding the formation of rainbows. Each color is characteristic of a distinct wave frequency, and different frequencies will bend in varying amounts upon passage through a prism. *Merriam-Webster's* defines bending as "to yield by curving as from pressure; to give in; to yield." That definition is similar to the statement about the dispersion of light. Frequencies can also refract different amounts when passing through a spectrum. Refract means "to turn aside, to break, to cause a ray of light to undergo bending." These words describe what was going on in my heart and life where no one could see. Visible light passed through the prism of my heart. The colors were not brilliant; they were shadows and shades, blackness and dark.

Yes, my physical body had been harmed, but that which

penetrated my heart and soul bent and broke me in other ways. It is very tough to mold a piece of steel. It has to become red-hot under the pressure of fire to make it form into the desired image.

Words can speak life or death. The words used, the tone conveyed, and the intensity of the words can leave a person feeling quite helpless. One may lash back with words of one's own, but the impact is like a knife piercing the heart.

Shared and unshared incidents of my life have formed me as they passed through a prism. False beliefs convinced me that I had to meet certain standards to feel good about myself. I craved approval from others. I believed I was unworthy of love and deserved to be punished. I was what I was; I could not change, so I was hopeless.

These were my beliefs, and they were fed by a lifetime diet of other people's opinions. I became stuck in the performance trap. I feared failure. I needed approval and feared rejection. I was ready to lose myself at any cost to please people. I was overly sensitive to criticism. Anything said in fun or in truth was an attack on me. I withdrew emotionally and physically from people to avoid disapproval. I blamed others out of fear of punishment; I withdrew from God. Shame filled my life. I lived in hopelessness; I felt inferior most of the time. I became passive. I did not dare to be creative. I was isolated in spirit.

I tried to avoid failure at all costs. This was how I explained the failure to myself. I climbed a tall ladder, met every expectation along the way. I saw the goal, and in my excitement to achieve the prize, my foot missed the top rung of the ladder, and I slid all the way down to the bottom, knowing I had to try again and again. After a time, one knows one will never achieve, and finally one agrees with what others have been saying all along: "You are a loser. You will never amount to anything in your life."

My heart was full of anger and resentment because of the pain I experienced in my life. I believe most of my life was lived in a state of depression. It is said that anger is despair turned inward. I saw no hope for change. I doubted I could make a wise decision. The fear of making a mistake paralyzed me from making decisions.

I saw everything in living color but in a negative, suppressed way. I hated myself, my parents, and God. My world was full of negativity. I was engulfed in anger, hate, and rejection. I could see no good in my world.

Psalms 107:33–36 (NASB) says, "He changes rivers into wilderness, and springs of water into a thirsty ground; a fruitful land into salt waste, because of the wickedness of those who dwell in it. He changes a wilderness into a pool of water, and a dry land into springs of water, and there He makes the hungry dwell, so that they may establish an inhabited city." The verses teach us that God allows certain circumstances and experiences in our lives to show us how to depend upon Him. We experience the results of our anger and pain; but when we change our heart's attitude and recognize Him as Lord and Savior of our lives, He establishes and gives us His resources to succeed.

I could easily give love, but it was hard for me to receive it. I found it difficult to reveal my inner thoughts and motives because I believed that people would reject me if they really knew what I was like. My intense fear of rejection caused me to form superficial relationships that led to isolation. The more one experiences loneliness, the more one needs acceptance to get what one needs. Eric Fromm once wrote in *The Search for Significance*, "The deep need of man is the need to overcome separateness, to leave the prison of his aloneness."

Through my growing up years, I learned to harden my

defenses in anticipation of being rejected again and again. Rejection became a form of communication for me. Rejection conveyed a message that one does not measure up to something that has been created or adopted. This can be used and seen as manipulation designed to control someone. It can be an outburst of anger, a disgusted look, a social snub, or an impatient answer. Whatever form it comes in, it communicates disrespect and a lack of appreciation and it implies low value. One can send a message almost immediately that his or her standards have not been met. I have been guilty of this many times with people, including my kids and grandkids, just as it was enacted upon me.

Many times in my life, when someone asked me to do a project or a job, I immediately said yes because I strived to gain approval. I would rarely turn anyone down, yet inside I was anxious and fearful; I really did not want to carry out the request. It was a terrible place to be. Galatians 1:10 (AMP) sums up this behavior: "Now am I trying to win the favor of me, or of God? Do I seek to please men? If I were still seeking popularity with me, I should not be a bond servant of Christ (the Messiah)."

That was me to a tee! I was hopelessly running on a wheel and never getting anywhere. I did not know how to jump off and live in freedom, let alone freedom in Christ.

Shame was paramount in my life. I had a poor self-image. I was always told by my dad that I should have been a boy. He said, "You would have been a great football player or a great basketball player if you had been a boy." How could I become a boy when I was a girl? He also made references to my weight. I weighed 108 pounds out of high school. I genuinely don't know why I did not have an eating disorder. In a time when one's body is changing due to puberty, these remarks can wound. Self-image reflects who we think we are and how everyone else sees us. We often believe what others say about us as gospel. We often believe what the world tells us regarding ideas, philosophies, and thoughts. We build our fortresses around these worldviews. Paul, in 2 Corinthians 10:4–5, tells us how to combat these thoughts. We must take these thoughts captive to the obedience of Christ. We must tell ourselves the truth, not the lies.

Even after I was married, I was scrutinized and felt rejected by my parents because they did not approve of my husband. My parents disapproved of the number of children we had, my husband's work, his family, and our activities. They would always tell me all the things my husband did or did not do. We were not raising our children according to their standards. Even though I was married and on my own, I was still bound by their expectations. They disliked and criticized everything my husband did.

As a family, we could never compete with my brother and his family. My brother and his wife received my parents' affection and approval. My brother was always successful, and my husband was a misfit. My brother was performance oriented like my folks were, and my husband was not. My brother and his wife seemed to sense the unspoken competition, and they pitted us against Dad and Mom. There was always something wrong with our family. We were an embarrassment to my parents, but my brother and his wife were perfect.

It seemed I was a thorn in my mother's side. She seemed embarrassed by me; I was sloppy in comparison to her perfectionism. I appeared to shame her if everything was not exactly in its place. When she came to visit our home when our kids were young, the first thing she would do (after I cleaned the whole house in preparation for their arrival) was to tell me how filthy the house was. She then spent the entire time cleaning my house from top to bottom. I should have welcomed that, but it was an insult to me. There was never a time when mother and daughter simply sat and talked or experienced the joy of playing with the grandchildren. It was always about cleanliness. Even though we never bridged the gap in my growing up years, I'd expected we would be on the same page when I married. How silly of me to presume this!

My parents decided to spend their winters in the Southwest in the 1980s. They would leave before Thanksgiving and would return in April. We did go see them the year that my husband broke his leg, but they never asked us to stay. They lived in a gated community where no kids were allowed, and we were told that the kids would make too much noise. We understood that we were not welcome in their world.

Although they had the time and money to visit us, they never broke away to celebrate birthdays or go to school functions while they were in the Southwest. From the time our daughter was little, they never visited to celebrate her birthday and she remembers that to this day.

When my folks had their twenty-fifth wedding anniversary, many people told me what great parents I had. I stood amazed as they shared how my parents had given of themselves to help others, how generous they were with their time and resources, and how encouraging they had always been. Many said they were the perfect couple in our hometown; no one had a better name or character. My thoughts were conflicted when I heard these things, and I asked myself, *Where were those parents in our lives?*

I know people change. I did see that change as they aged, but so many years were lost between us regarding who they were when growing up versus who they were with others. I saw it as a loss and a tragedy.

My parents were always worried about their good name, and they held to a strict standard regarding it. They insisted that their kids and grandkids perform well around others too. My brother and his family met the bill, but our family were outcasts, and we were never accepted in their circle. We tried, but we never measured up to the unseen expectations that shadowed us.

One year around Thanksgiving, we called to ask my folks if we could come down to spend the holiday with them because my husband was able to get off work. I was told that my brother and his family were coming, and it would be too much for them to share themselves with both families. They told us not to come, so we did not go. It hurt me beyond words and drove home the belief that we were indeed unloved and unwanted.

There were oil wells drilled on our farm, and each of us received a share of the revenue from them. Our checks were large every month. My husband loved motorcycles, and I loved to ride with him. With one of the large oil checks, I decided to buy him a motorcycle. He was thrilled.

He had his motorcycle sitting in front of the house when, out of the blue and without warning, my parents made a surprise visit. My dad saw this rare beauty and became instantly angry at me. He told me that he was sorry he'd given me a share of the oil. He said if this was how I was going to spend my money, it was a waste for him to give it to me. I got up from the table and went to my bedroom, where there were two oil checks on my dresser. I took the checks and slammed them down in front of him, saying that I did not want money that came with conditions. I had never stood up to my dad before, and he was shocked by my response. I told him that if I was going to be scrutinized as to how I chose to spend a gift, then it was not a gift to begin with. The oil checks remained in my possession.

I share this to show how I was able to break free from my prison. That day became Freedom Day. I stood up and faced the giant. I looked him in the eye. The chains were broken. It was the day I stepped away from the lies and began to tell myself the truth.

I believed many lies about myself from many sources, and these lies caused great shame. Lies and guilt are like an oil spill in an ocean. As it hits the beach, it forms a tarlike substance. If our feet touch it, they become stained, and we wonder if we will ever get rid of that stain from our feet. Shame is like oil and is the emotional tar of our lives. It takes an act of God to rid us of the stains we feel in our hearts and lives. This was my beginning.

Life and circumstances change people. Those experiences turned me upside down too. I have struggled most of my life with feeling insecure, inadequate, awkward, uncomfortable, inferior, abandoned, and rejected. Most of those memories and life experiences will be with me the rest of my life. Thankfully, the Lord has not abandoned me. Hebrews 13:5b (AMP) says it so clearly: "Be satisfied with your present [circumstances and with what you have]; for He [God] Himself has said, *I will not* in any way fail you nor give you up nor leave you without support. (*I will not, [I will] not, [I will not* in any degree leave you helpless nor forsake nor let [you] down (relax My hold on you)! [Assuredly not!]" Wow! I am amazed. No one in human flesh stands by like God does! We have His promise that He will not fail or leave us without support. He emphatically says, "He will not!"

Titus 3:3–7 (AMP) states these truths.

> For we also were once thoughtless and senseless, obstinate and disobedient and misled; [we too were once] slaves to all sorts of cravings and

pleasures, wasting our days in malice and jealousy and envy, hateful (hated, detestable) and hating one another. But when the goodness and loving-kindness of God our Savior to man [as man] appeared, He saved us, not because of His own pity and mercy, by [the] cleansing [bath] of the new birth (regeneration) and renewing of the Holy Spirit which He poured out [so] richly upon us through Jesus Christ our Savior. [And He did it in order] that we might be justified by His grace (by His favor, wholly undeserved), [that we might be acknowledged and counted as conformed to the divine will in purpose, thought, and action], and that we might become heirs of eternal life according to our hope.

Those verses were my hope, my transformation, my redemption, my renewal, my justification, and my regeneration in Jesus Christ.

Sandi Patti sings a song called "You Call Me Yours." Some of the words are, "Your voice it covers all my shame, the old turned to new. No matter how things look to me. You see a destiny, a perfect promise. It's hard for me to understand exactly what You see. I slip and stumble everyday but still You say believe. You see me for my heart and not the bruises. You call me beautiful … You call me Yours."

It is not how we see ourselves but how Jesus sees us: beautiful, holy, worthy, forgiven, and righteous. The song tells me who I really am based on Jesus Christ's perspective. I have His name and His inheritance. I am His. I am cherished and loved beyond my own belief. Thank you, Jesus.

Prism—Jesus's Light

A prism is a triangular piece of glass that allows light to spread out into a band of seven colors. These colors are red, orange, yellow, green, indigo, blue, and violet. Isaac Newton discovered that sunshine (white light) is made up of many colors when he passed a beam of light through a prism. A prism is transparent.

I was eighteen when I accepted Jesus Christ into my life. In fact, I received Him many times because I was taught to not believe in eternal security. In other words, I had thought that if I did wrong and did not have time to confess that wrong to Jesus before I died, I was going to hell. My whole life was filled with anxiety and fear because I was always doing something wrong. My acceptance of Jesus at eighteen was the beginning of a beautiful change. However, it took about twenty more years for Christ to change me to the point where I could honor Him with my life entirely.

In between those years, I struggled with life, memories, and beliefs, and at one point I almost walked away from my faith. I had looked evil in the face more than once, and it was ugly. Sometimes we cannot forgive ourselves for the choices and decisions we have made in our lives; those choices become dirty ashes, a reminder of the past. Past sins and memories enslave us to the point that we cannot break the power of sin in our lives. My choices and decisions became a chain that made me a prisoner, bruised me, and held me fast.

My four years working in a Christian organization helped me study God's Word and encouraged me to thirst for more. After I married, I was involved in Bible studies, and my thirst for God continued to grow. Psalm 1:3 (NLT) states, "They are like trees planted along the riverbank, bearing fruit each season. Their leaves never wither, and they prosper in all they do."

I was encouraged by our pastor to become a counselor. I started training in Colorado, but first I had to go through some intense counseling myself. I received a diploma for my studies and went on to pursue my college degree. I graduated and received a bachelor of arts degree in psychology. I worked in various churches doing counseling. I loved it. I had finally found my niche. I continued counseling for many years until the laws of Nebraska changed. I started my master's program but did not complete it due to further changes in the regulations.

When I started my training in Colorado, I learned who I was in Jesus Christ. He did not just save me—He regenerated me, changed me, broke the power of sin in my life, and renewed me. I was alive to God, and this seemed unbelievable to me. I had lacked a real understanding of God before I learned these truths because my whole belief system in God had been skewed. How could this God love me without conditions? If I slapped Him in the face, He would still love me. Incredible! If I failed Him daily, He would always love me. Unbelievable! Who was this God? I knew Him from a distance, I believed in Him, and I trusted in Him with the biblical principles, but my heart was far from Him.

I believed He was a God who carried a big stick, ready to pop me whenever I got out of line. However, he wasn't; He was nothing like my earthly father. He wanted me to have an intimate relationship as His daughter and His friend. The close relationship I had with my dad was hurtful; God was asking me to trust Him explicitly. His link to me would be one of love and acceptance despite how I saw myself. He wanted to teach me all about Himself and how to repair the damage that had occurred in my life. His whole aim was love. I had never known love like that.

He had to change my thoughts and beliefs from the inside out. He had to retrain my mind to believe that His Words were right. He died for me, and He wanted me to experience His love, grace, and forgiveness in His way. He saw me worthy to be His child. He offered me freedom from sin and His power to conquer sin. In other words, He had equipped me with His resources, His love, and His strength so I would never walk alone again. He will never reject me. His arms are always opened wide to accept me just as I am. These lessons are illustrated by only God. Micah 6:8 (AMP) tells us His requirements, "He has shown you, o man, what is good. And what does the Lord require of you, but to do justly, and to love kindness and mercy, and to humble yourself and walk humbly with your God." It is illustrated again in Deuteronomy 10:12 (AMP) when the Lord tells the nation Israel what He requires of them: "But [reverently] to fear the Lord your God, [that is] to walk in all His ways and to love Him, and to serve the Lord your God with all your [mind and] heart and with your entire being."

After what God had accomplished in me, how could I not give Him my whole life? He broke the chains of sin that held me fast. He loved me regardless of the blemishes of sin in me. He gave me a new heart to feast on Him. He gave me His forgiveness so that I may forgive others. He showed me mercy when I should have received an indictment. Who does that but God?

He made His child, a daughter, to enjoy all the blessings of His family. He cleansed me from all my impurities. I have a new position in me—from darkness into light, from slave to daughter, from sin to righteousness, from death to life, from inadequacy to abundance in Him, from physical death to eternal life, from weakness to unexplainable power in Christ, from rags to riches, from dirtiness to purity, from hate to love, from anger to joy, from agitation to soul peace. He gave me so much. How could I not give Him myself for His service?

My life has changed because of what Christ accomplished for me on the cross. Second Corinthians 5:17 (AMP) states, "Therefore, if any person is [ingrafted] in Christ (the Messiah) he is a new creation (a new creature altogether); the old [previous moral and spiritual condition) has passed away. Behold, the fresh and new has come." When He was buried, I was in Him, and when He rose again, I rose from sin and death to new life in Him. He is interceding for me in Heaven. I can never repay Him, but out of gratitude I try to live for Him, tell others about His mercy and grace, and choose to pattern my life after Him. I owe Him my life.

When I accepted these words into my heart, I was no longer Ann the sinner—I became Ann the saint. I had a name change, and I was new from the inside out. I received a new life, a new beginning, a new position, and a new master–Jesus Christ.

I saw Jesus. It did not matter what I had done before because now I saw Jesus, and my life was changed.

He knew me through the scars and loved me still. Nothing in this life matters more than Jesus. It is my desire to honor Him with my life. How can I say thanks for all He has done for me? Only by living for Him is my prayer. To God be the glory for all He has accomplished for us.

He wanted to do work from the inside out so I would know freedom in Christ. In the beginning, I had many false beliefs, and I was still listening to the lies from the past. He wanted me to change those beliefs. First, I had to recognize them as lies and change my thoughts to mirror what He says in the Scripture.

False beliefs ruled my life. What I had endured as a child formed my feelings about myself. My thoughts were tied to my emotions, and the two worked together to produce actions. For example, when I was abused, my feelings told me I was hated, alone, and rejected. I felt that intensely.

God had a better plan based on truth from His perspective. If we base our thoughts on God, we will have godly thoughts, which lead to healthy emotions and then godly actions. God's truth is based on the Word of God. As I read the scriptures, the Holy Spirit transforms my thoughts into godly thoughts, which lead me to experience peace, joy, love, patience, gentleness, kindness, self-control, self-restraint, goodness, and humility (Galatians 5:22–23). In other words, these are the fruits of His Spirit living in me. It produces healthy emotions which then generates godly actions.

In the old system of beliefs, I had to think, feel, and act as my false beliefs dictated, but the day I accepted Jesus into my life was the day of righteousness—a right way of thinking, being, and living. I became a new creation the very moment these truths became facts in my heart.

I am completely forgiven. I am righteous and pleasing to

God. I am totally accepted. I am deeply loved. I am complete in Jesus; I am His child. I am a Christ-One, and the Holy Spirit resides in me.

These truths are what I longed for all of my life—to have identity and to know I belonged to someone. I was loved, forgiven, and now a part of the family of God.

It has been a learning curve for me as my past comes to threaten me with new revelations and memories, yet God continues to give me new truths in His Word that tells me that He will never leave, forsake, or abandon me; He will provide for what I lack, and I will join Him in heaven someday.

I was broken, and yet He saw me and redeemed me. It takes an act of our will and faith to put these truths into action. We must counteract the lies with His truth.

We all have believed lies told to us by sin, Satan, and our flesh. Those lies are beliefs we carry about ourselves. It can be through performance and others' opinions, or the belief we must meet certain criteria to be accepted by others and feel good about ourselves. These are false beliefs and lies. All these false beliefs bring hopelessness, rejection, and fear to our lives.

God wants us to see ourselves through His truth—who we are in Him. He tells us how deeply loved we are. We are forgiven. He accepts us based upon His death, burial, and resurrection. For me, a transformation has been completed, and I lack nothing. I am complete in Him.

When I began to learn these truths, I would be triggered by memories, insecurities, pain, condemnation, fear, and rejection. God's Word was my help. Romans 6:11 (NLT) says, "So you also should consider yourselves to be dead to the power of sin and alive to God through Christ Jesus." In other words, whenever those negative thoughts came, I needed to tell myself I was no longer under sin's power. I needed to make a shift and place them in their rightful place: under God's dominion and control. I am alive to God just as He says in His Word. It goes on to say in Romans 6:12–13 that we are not to allow sin to rule (to make its home in us) any longer or to subject ourselves to the cravings of lusts and passions. "Sin is no longer your master, for you no longer live under the requirements of the law. Instead, you live under the freedom of God's grace" (Romans 6:14 NLT).

When I sin now, I have a choice to once again be ruled by sin, or I can choose to allow Christ to rule my heart. As the scripture began to unfold these truths, I saw how His brilliant light conquered the darkness of my soul.

My life verses are found in Philippians 3:8–10, and they bear my commitment to know Him intimately. It was His love that inspired a crumpled up little girl to dare to trust a loving God who changed her heart and life from the inside out. Without His love, I would be a ship without a sail, aimlessly floating without purpose or plan. My words cannot express the deep love I have for my Lord and Savior for rescuing me. I was in the blackest of mire, and He placed me into Him so that I might live purposely and in His power. Thank You, Jesus. Thank You!

The desire of my heart is to be like Jesus. He is my hope and vision. I pray that He will always be my vision no matter what comes my way.

John Newton's song "Amazing Grace" tells of how God changed him. Grace is mentioned six times in the four stanzas. John Newton needed grace as he remembered all the things he had done in his past. The apostle Paul also knew about grace when he said in 1 Corinthians 15:9–10 (NASB), "For I am the least of the apostles, who am not fit to be called an apostle, because I persecuted the church of God. But by the grace of God, I am what

I am, and His grace toward me did not prove vain; but I labored even more than all of them, yet not I, but the grace of God with me." His grace is redemptive mercy for the recipient. God's grace overshadowed all the evil of John Newton's life, Paul's life, my life, and countless others' lives.

The Brilliant Light of Jesus Christ's Prism

A RAINBOW IS CAUSED BY THE RAYS OF THE SUN REFLECTING FROM falling raindrops at an angle to the eye of the spectator. A beautiful arch of mirrored and refracted light is formed for every eye. Although the rainbow spans a continuous spectrum of colors, we only see the rainbow in seven distinct colors, which may have a spiritual significance. Those seven colors are red, orange, yellow, green, blue, indigo, and violet. The number seven represents completion and perfection, so the rainbow pictures God's perfect plan. When all the colors of the rainbow are combined, they give us white sunlight. White is the symbol of purity and the righteousness of Christ, just as black (the opposite of white) pictures sin.

The first acknowledgment of a rainbow is in Genesis 9. God had just flooded the whole earth and destroyed wickedness, but He'd saved Noah and his family in the ark. God made a covenant that was universal to all generations, and it was a sign of a rainbow in the sky. It formed an arc across the expanse for all to see. When the clouds cleared, light refraction showed this beautiful display.

The Hebrew word for *rainbow* is also the word for a battle bow. In Old Testament times, God referred to judgment storms by using bows and arrows. The bow is now "put away," hung in place by the clouds, suggesting that the "battle" is over. The bow now means peace. The rainbow would be used in the Israelites' lives as a strengthening tool, which shows that God keeps His promises of grace. It also reminded them that God's judgment was completed for this age. During the end-time or when Jesus returns, judgment will come again.

Colors are clearly seen through Jesus Christ's prism. I would like to suggest a possible spiritual significance contained in the rainbow.

Red represents the blood of Jesus Christ, His shed blood for us. It means our redemption. It stands for the price that has been paid (Romans 5:8).

Orange is a combination of red and yellow, which is symbolic of God's divine nature and His sacrificial love. God did not even spare His own Son; God gave His Son up for us all (John 3:16).

Yellow is the color of glory. It represents eternal life and Christ's life (John 8:12; Romans 6:23).

Green represents man's perfect environment in the Garden of Eden. It is the color of plant life. It could stand for longevity, eternity, or earthly prosperity. John 15 talks about the vine and the branches. The plant life—its health—is strictly dependent upon it abiding in the vine. It must be in union with the tree, or it will never survive or bear fruit.

Blue is the color of the sky. It reminds us of God's faithfulness. The blue color of the heavens does not change, neither does God. It also refers to the righteousness of God (Malachi 3:6; John 6:38).

Indigo is a deep violet blue. It is slightly blue with a reddish cast to it. This could represent our Lord Jesus Christ as a propitiation for our sins. "And He Himself is the propitiation (satisfaction) for our sins; and not for ours only, but also for those of the whole world" (1 John 2:2 NASB).

Violet is the last of the colors. Violet is the color in the rainbow with the shortest wavelength and is considered a shade of purple. Purple is the color of kings and is symbolic of royalty. "But you are a CHOSEN RACE, A ROYAL PRIESTHOOD, A HOLY NATION, A PEOPLE FOR GOD'S OWN POSSESSION, that you may proclaim the excellencies of Him who has called you out of darkness into His marvelous light" (1 Peter 2:9 NASB).

We are God's people. He is our family. We are to pattern our lives after Him.

British evangelist Henry Varley said in 1873 in Dublin, "The world has yet to see what God can do with and for and through and in a man who is fully and wholly consecrated in Him." I want to be that person who is totally useable to my Lord and Savior.

This is my story—a story of brokenness, shadows, and shades. Yet now I enjoy the many colors of the rainbows and the brilliant light of Jesus Christ in my life. It is all about knowing Jesus. He is my all. He is my hope and my legacy.

I pray that all who read this booklet will be able to identify what was accomplished for us on the cross and all that we possess in Jesus Christ. In 1741, George Frederic Handel penned these words to "Worthy is the Lamb."

Thank You for the cross, Lord. Thank You for the price You paid. Bearing all my sin and shame, in love You came and gave amazing grace.

Thank You for this love, Lord. Thank You for the nail pierced hands. washed me in Your cleansing flow, now all I know Your forgiveness and embrace.

> Worthy is the Lamb, seated on the throne. Crown You now with many crowns. You reign victorious. High and lifted up, Jesus Son of God. The darling of heaven crucified, Worthy is the Lamb, Worthy is the Lamb.

My Hope

As you have read this book, I hope you have been challenged to understand my testimony of faith in Jesus Christ. God has given us eternal life. It is a gift. For us to experience eternal life is to acknowledge several things.

There is a chasm between us and God. Sin separates us. God is holy, and His standard is righteousness. We are told in Romans 3:23, "For all have sinned and fall short of the glory of God" (NASB).

Second, there is no amount of "goodness" we can do to obtain acceptance with God that will get us into heaven. Ephesians 2:8–9 tells us that it is grace that we are saved through faith in His death, burial, and resurrection. It has nothing to do with our goodness or our works, morality, or religious activities. It is the gift of God. It is not because of our works that we are saved.

God's plan is love and grace. Romans 5:8 (NASB) tells us, "But God demonstrates His own love toward us, in that while we were sinners, Christ died for us."

This is God's good news to us. He sent His own son to die on the cross for our sin. He shed his blood for every sin that has ever been committed. He then rose from the dead, proving that death had no hold on Him, and He was our substitution. "He who was delivered up because of our transgressions, and was raised because of our justification" (Romans 4:25 NASB).

How do we receive God's Son? "But to all who believed him and accepted him, he gave the right to become children of God" (John 1:12 NLT).

We must realize we are sinners. We realize that nothing we do will gain salvation, and we must realize that we must totally rely on Jesus by faith for our salvation. There is an action on our part. We must believe. Romans 10:9 states, "That if you *confess* your mouth Jesus as Lord, and *believe* in your heart that God raised Him from the dead, *you shall be saved;* for with the heart man believes resulting in righteousness, and the mouth he confesses, resulting in salvation" (NASB; emphasis mine).

The moment you receive Jesus into your heart this is what happens: "Therefore is any man is in Christ, he is a new creature; the old things passed away; behold, new things have come" (2 Corinthians 5:17 NASB).

If you feel God tugging on your heart to make this decision, please pray this simple prayer.

> I know I am a sinner, and I ask for forgiveness. I believe Jesus Christ is Your Son. I believe He died for my sin and that He rose from the dead. I want to trust Him as my Savior and follow Him as Lord of my life from this day forward. Guide me and teach me in Your ways, and help me to do Your will. Thank You for loving and accepting me into Your family. I pray this in the name of Jesus. Amen.

To my fellow brothers and sisters in Christ: I know that trust is a huge factor in any type of abuse. It is very difficult to trust people, let alone a mighty God. We do see through rose-colored glasses. Everything in our lives have been distorted from the simple to the complex. We lost many things to abuse. We all have triggers of some sort that we don't always understand. Nevertheless, God wants us to strip away our self-control and our defenses and to trust Him unreservedly. It will take practice to do so because we need to replace lies with His truth as seen in the Word of God.

Identity is everything in our lives. How we identify ourselves plays a huge part in our health and healing. God wants us to be victors, not victims. He does not want us to see ourselves as unworthy; He wants us to see ourselves as beautiful. That is how He sees us.

Metamorphosis shows us a process of transformation, from a worm to a butterfly. Just as in nature, God does for us in our abuse. He changes the ugly into the beautiful. We are not those people anymore. We have new lives in Christ! The old is gone, and the new has come.

Pour over the scriptures. Bathe yourself in them. The scriptures will be your help, your strength, and your companion when those crazy times bear down upon your emotions.

God has not abandoned us, though it may feel that way at times. Hebrews 13:5b–6 in the Amplified Bible are powerful words when our worlds are out of control and we feel abandoned and forsaken. We must tell ourselves the truth. God is there. He has not failed us.

And be satisfied with your present [circumstances and with what you have]; for He [God] Himself has said, I will not, [I will] not, [I will] not in any degree leave you helpless nor forsake nor let [you] down (relax My hold on you)! [Assuredly not!] So we take comfort and are encouraged and confidently and boldly say, The Lord is My Helper; I will not be seized with alarm [I will not fear or dread or be terrified]. What can man do to me?

Our journey from abuse is a difficult one, but we must keep our focus on the Lord Jesus Christ. We are no longer captives— we are free in Christ. Some things will always be remembered, but when those times come, let us lay them at the cross and carry them no more.

Let us change our perspective, our identity, and our victimization into victory. Put your armor on (Ephesians 6) and be freedom fighters!

Hebrews 12:1–3 (AMP) states,

> Therefore then, since we are surrounded by so great a cloud of witnesses [who have borne testimony to the Truth], let us strip off and throw aside every encumbrance (unnecessary weight) and that sin which so readily (deftly and cleverly) clings to and entangles us, and let us run with patient endurance and steady and active persistence the appointed course of the race that is set before us. Looking away [from all that will distract] to Jesus. Who is the Leader and the Source of our faith [giving the first incentive for our belief] and is also its Finisher [bringing it to maturity and perfection]. He, for the joy [of obtaining the prize] that was set before Him, endured the Cross, despising and ignoring the shame, and is now seated at the right hand of the throne of God. Just think of Him Who endured

from sinners such grievous opposition and bitter hostility against Himself [reckon up and consider it all in comparison with your trials], so that you may not grow weary or exhausted, losing heart and relaxing and fainting in your minds.

If we would pattern our lives after these verses and our Lord, we would have much hope.

Remember that we are lovely and beautiful to our Lord and Savior. We have a new name: Christ-One, beloved, a royal priesthood, a son or daughter of the King. Let us so live in the courts of the King, enjoying all the benefits and resources we have in Him.

Sincerely in Him,

Elaine Lewis

Printed in the United States
By Bookmasters